Do Listen

Understand what's really being said.
Find a new way forward.

Bobette Buster

CHRONICLE BOOKS
SAN FRANCISCO

First published in the United States of America in 2018 by Chronicle
Books LLC.

First published in the United Kingdom in 2018 by The Do Book
Company.

Text copyright © Bobette Buster 2018
Illustrations copyright © Erica Frances George 2018

Library of Congress Cataloging-in-Publication Data available.

ISBN 978-1-4521-7168-5

Manufactured in China.

MIX
Paper from
responsible sources
FSC™ C136333

Cover design by James Victore.
Book designed and set by Ratiotype.

10 9 8 7 6 5 4 3 2 1

Chronicle Books LLC
680 Second Street
San Francisco, California 94107
www.chroniclebooks.com

To my mother, Shirley.

The greatest listener I have ever known. Quiet, nonjudgmental, ever kind, she was *always* available to listen. And she did it so well, creating a common good in her everyday life. As my father said about her shortly before he passed, "I never heard an unkind word said about her."

Contents

No story lives unless someone wants to listen.

—

J. K. Rowling

Prologue

As a child, I was insatiably curious. The storytelling in my small world was wondrous, and I was always delighted to listen. I didn't want to miss a thing. I'd be sent to bed or out of the room, but then I'd tiptoe back down the stairs to listen at the crack of the door. My mother would find me asleep at the bottom of the staircase.

Or I would crawl under my grandmother's grand dining table and curl up into a ball so no one would know I was there. Then I'd experience 360 degrees of true surround sound. I heard the hilarity and the poetic, ironic quips of my family—their grace with language, witty asides, rhythmic cadences. All this rang out above and around me.

Introduction

> You cannot truly listen to anyone and do anything else at the same time.

M. Scott Peck, *The Road Less Traveled*

Over the past twenty-five years, I've listened to well over ten thousand stories as both a film production executive and story consultant, and while also lecturing in film school courses and facilitating storytelling workshops all over the world. When I first began this career, my intention was simply to listen to each story. Did the narrative work? How could it be improved? I had to learn the right questions to ask of both the story and the storyteller. But over time, I began to observe that when I was listening to the best stories—most often in a workshop setting—there was something deeper going on.

The storyteller possesses a powerful need—an *urge*—to tell their story. It's personal to them. And there is often a point in a well-told story when everyone in the room leans in. We quietly give the storyteller all the time they need to tell the full tale. We're actively listening.

As their story shifts, the room shifts. We are all ears, listening with full attention, as if gathered around a campfire. A bond develops. As the story comes to a close, inexorably, we are changed—as the story has indeed changed the storyteller. And, in the end, our listening resonates in palpable heartfelt connections. And, yes, it's emotional: tears, outbursts of laughter, smiles. People reach out to each other. And invariably they say, "Wow." They usually have no adequate words for the experience.

In one such group of about fifteen entrepreneurs—leaders in their fields, each successful in their own right—I gathered everyone around a table, effectively creating a story circle. I began by asking one simple question: "Tell us something about yourself that we would otherwise never know." Their answers vary widely, of course, and some are very personal. But, I tell them, this is not therapy. I am mostly there to curate the time, so that everyone in the group has a chance to share. I monitor the experience carefully.

The first couple of stories are usually not very substantive as, of course, the participants do not want to embarrass themselves. But, invariably, over the course of the session, someone shares a profound story. I've never known this *not* to happen. Why? Because I think people long to tell their stories, and they just haven't had the right opportunity to be *heard*. Often, it's only in the process of the telling that they discover why the story matters to them.

To give you an example, the following story experience has long resonated with me.

Tom was a trim man in his fifties, dressed in jeans with a smart shirt and sweater. An upper-level executive, he had spent more than twenty years at a major communications company. He was attending the workshop with several colleagues.

On this day, Tom was the third one to speak. True to form, after the first two participants shared incidental personal stories, Tom spoke freely when it was his turn.

He said that he had left home young, around fourteen years old, and led a peripatetic life. He earned enough money through odd jobs to party each weekend, which usually meant getting stoned or drunk with his friends. This went on for years until early one Monday morning, when he was twenty-nine, Tom woke up in a diner booth and realized he'd been on a four-day bender. He couldn't even remember what had happened. Total blackout. It was then that he decided he was done with drinking. He didn't want this life anymore. Tom ended his story there. Job done, he assumed his turn was over. He had answered the exercise objective: he had told a story out loud that we would otherwise never have known.

The room was poleaxed. We did not expect this story from the healthy-looking, successful man in our midst. But I knew there was more to be heard. So rather than moving on to the next person, I simply asked, "What time of day was it when you woke up?"

He reflected, "Around ten in the morning."

I continued, "What did you see?"

"I remember there was this god-awful floor polisher cleaning the floor all around me. Just a terrible drone. And there was that sick-sweet smell of cleaning—all the tables and plastic booths—going on all around me. And they'd opened the windows; the morning light was knifing through. They were cleaning all around me. Who knows how long I'd been there?"

"What did you do next?"

"I went outside in the bright light and found a phone booth. That was when they had those Yellow Pages hanging in a thick book. I found the number for Alcoholics Anonymous. Someone answered. All I remember is that they took down my address, said I should go home, and they would send someone over for me that day to take me to a meeting."

"And what did you do when you got home?"

"I tore through my house and found every bottle—and poured out all the contents. Wherever they were stashed, under the sink, wherever. I flushed them all down the toilet. And then I sat down and waited."

"And . . . did someone come?"

"Yes, I remember sitting by the radiator watching the sun go down, waiting until about five."

"That was a long time to wait, wasn't it?"

"I don't remember. I was just so grateful they had promised a person would show up that day."

"And . . . ?"

"They did. They took me to my first meeting."

"And . . . now, twenty years on?"

"I never had another drink after that day."

Silence enveloped the room. Or, I should say, **listening**. Everyone's emotions were pent up to bursting. We were all tuned in to Tom. Why? Because he was so open—and vulnerable. How had this story of a young man who spoke of cleaning products, phone booths, and waiting by a radiator captured their attention?

Because there was another story quietly sitting behind the first one. I knew that if he could simply make us see the world as he saw it that day—in all its boring, prosaic details—that we would be there with him. The true story would reveal itself. So I asked: "How was it that you'd spent almost half your life—from age fourteen to age twenty-nine—without any apparent direction or training for a better job, and you'd become an alcoholic? What are the odds that someone like that would pick themselves up and choose to change? What made this day of all days different?"

Tom looked away and said, "I don't know why I told this story today. You know, I've never told anyone this story." His colleagues nodded in astonishment. "I don't know why I did today."

But I knew it was because Tom *needed* to tell the story of the moment when he took control of his life. *Carpe diem.* When he discovered his own courage. Young, twenty-nine-year-old Tom, who had spent half his life "locked out of his brain," had made a simple, clear-cut choice to do something he'd never done before. He acknowledged he needed help, and let go. This was an act of great bravery.

Why did he tell this story, in full, on this day? Because I simply listened and asked active memory questions that appealed to the senses. Ordinary ones. What did you see? What time of day was it? What did you hear? What did you do next? Ordinary details—cleaning smells, the floor-buffer drone, the Yellow Pages, flushing a toilet, sitting by a radiator—all this, the dull stuff of life, make us all connect. And in the ordinary, we can now expect the extraordinary to happen.

These are Sense Memories. I asked the group afterward, "What one detail first comes to mind when you remember Tom's story?" Most said the Yellow Pages, or the bright yellow morning sun and how he sat until the sunset and the AA friend arrived. The color yellow encompassed them all. I call this the Gleaming Detail—because in that one detail, the entire story comes alive.

I asked the group to tell me what they responded to, even though I knew their answers would come down to the moment of Tom's active choice. When he found the Yellow Pages, he was choosing to find help. And he did. Tom was revealing a moment of profound personal courage. The thing about sharing a personal story about courage is this: if I can visualize your act of courage, I am emboldened to discover my own courage, too. As Tom needed to tell his story, *we* needed to hear it. Courage is a spiritual muscle that, once activated, can stimulate the imaginations of other people and inspire them to make their own choices, too. We open our hearts to wonder. If we can hear and see it, we can be it. We can do it, too. In this book we'll hear more about how the act of listening can ennoble the listeners and be a catalyst for change.

From then on, the class blossomed into a full day of the participants sharing moments of fear and cowardice overcome, hilarious breakthroughs, or quiet revelation. By the end of the day, the group had bonded, and many had developed friendships that carry forward today. This is not an uncommon outcome of my sessions.

In the case of Tom's story, we listened to a man take up the courage one dreary Monday morning to grab hold of his life and never look back. We became strengthened and emboldened, just by the act of listening. In listening, we gave Tom the permission and space to speak aloud about what had been a closed part of his life. Imagine if we did this for other people we meet? What if each of us took the time to listen to just one other person in this way? And it doesn't have to be a stranger: what about our nearest and dearest?

Over time, I came to see that the act of listening had a transformative effect on anyone in the room. I could "hear" the shift in the room. I could feel the palpable connection—or, by contrast, the lack of interest when people stopped listening, the energy seeming to drain from the room like a balloon seeping air. As I tuned in to these experiences, I developed a kind of radar to feel the power of the story or to read the mood of a room— and I began to observe how I could orchestrate it for the better. All by listening.

The hidden world reveals itself when we listen.

This book is about rediscovering the lost art of listening, and then using that ability to form deeper connections and generate moments of wonder. Once you listen well to another person, you both connect. You are never the same again. We break through our own limitations and self-interest. Listening is the only way we can continue to grow and flourish as individuals—and as a society.

There is no greater agony than bearing an untold story in you.

Maya Angelou

My Process

All of us are living a story. And behind this, we have an untold story that we long to tell. But sometimes we don't yet know it, or know how to make ourselves heard.

Here are some pointers on how I have learned to listen and draw out these untold stories in my workshops, classes, and daily life.

My process is this: I take the time necessary, and I ask simple questions, to open up a common space between us.

— What happened next?

— What time of day was it? Where were you? What do you remember from that moment?

— Why do you think you did that?

These kinds of questions always elicit vivid memories and energize the storyteller's passion for the story.

Then, at the appropriate moment, I pause.

I acknowledge the storyteller's moment of courage—that moment when they made a significant change in their life—because *that* moment is inevitably why they have chosen to tell this story, though they typically didn't realize that was why, at least not at first.

As the storyteller becomes more relaxed, I embolden them by asking the following:

— How did you feel?

— How do you feel now?

Often, they are deeply moved—because in your listening to them, you have brought them out into a wider, more open space.

They have felt *heard*. There is great power is this act. A new trust has been born.

And if you are in a group setting, you will most certainly experience the unleashed desire for everyone else to want to be heard, too.

We have forgotten the
power of silence.

—

Bobette Buster

1
The Lost Art of Listening

Why is it we feel surprised, even grateful, when someone really hears us—when someone leans in and gives us their time and attention? How has this basic act and most primal of senses become such a rare commodity in today's world? Has the one-way street of social media "broadcasting" really marked the end of conversation and listening?

A national news channel recently conducted an experiment with a small group of teenagers between fourteen and sixteen years old—the generation sometimes known as "screenagers." The reporter's story was addressing the latest scientific studies that suggest smartphones encourage addictive behaviors, ADHD, depression, FOMO (fear of missing out), and so on. Her experiment was to see what would happen if she took away the teenagers' smartphones and laptops. They were to go cold turkey for one full week.

I expected that the teens would report great resentment, high anxiety, and frustration at being cut off. And, of course, some of them did. But they also knew this experiment had an end date, which likely mitigated some of those negative feelings. When they were asked how they felt at the end of the week, to the reporter's—and my own—surprise, all the students responded with what I call "curious wonder." They were slightly amazed at how much they enjoyed talking with their families over dinner. They found time for conversation with their friends. They got their homework done and finished their chores—much to their parents' amazement. It is often said that the smartphone has killed small talk, as well as the quiet ability to just hang out and learn to handle boredom. When the teens were asked what they took away from this week-long famine of social media connectivity, one fifteen-year-old girl said, "I really want to stop using my phone and learn to just *be* with my friends." Face to face. Not in a group with each person's face pressed into their individual screens. She was genuinely filled with a curious hope. Like she'd never encountered this thought before. What a novel idea!

It's interesting to note that when each of us was in our mother's womb, our eyes were closed but our ears already worked. We heard her heartbeat, the swishing of the amniotic fluid, and the jolt of loud noises in the outer world. That was our world. As such, our hearing is connected to our primal emotions and memories. Only when we are born do our eyes open, gather focus, and take in all the light and tonal differences of this new world. Since our eyes are on the front of our face, our main reference point from then on is visual—our perspective is usually based on whatever our eyes can see. Listening retreats to the periphery insofar as our perception is concerned. But it remains the ambient light of our emotions, hard-wired to our first feelings. From the time our ears are formed, they remain on, 24/7. Our hearing is our last sense to go when we die. This is why the Greeks said that our ears are the "guardian of our sleep." A mother will hear her baby cry in the dead of night.

Medical science has discovered that the minute hairs lining the cochlea in our ear canals contract and expand similar to the irises of our eyes. They expand and contract in response to sound waves coming in. Our ears are alerting and protecting us as best they can, but in modern times, indeed ever since the industrial age, our ears have been under assault. Now, we close our ears to all the overlapping, nonstop sonic intrusions. We are selective—choosing to block out the natural world with our headphones, empowered to choose what we want to hear. But in doing so, we are no longer able to sense what is calling us. We have lost the ability to listen. We have forgotten—if we ever knew—the power of silence. We cannot remember how the birds and animals speak—and why we even need to know what they are saying.

Before the industrial age—roughly the years between the mid-eighteenth and mid-nineteenth centuries—all humanity existed in a world filled with pastoral, natural sounds. In some cases, sound had a direct bearing on a family's livelihood, as in the case of, for instance, sheep farmers, who relied on the superior hearing of dogs to extend their own honed senses and keep their flocks safe from predators. In the towns, the community's news came from the sudden pealing of church bells ringing out from the tallest spire in the town center, gathering all together as one within its sonic range. The news was sometimes uplifting, sometimes somber. One would know which by the cadence of the bells' peal. (This tradition continued past the industrial age—when President John F. Kennedy was assassinated on November 22, 1963, England's Queen

Elizabeth I ordered that the bells of Westminster Abbey be soberly rung once every minute from 11 a.m. to noon in the following days—a solemn honor that had historically been reserved only for members of the royal family. When reminded of this fact, she simply commanded that the tolling of the Westminster bells be done. And they were.)

In London, there is a small, unique museum called Dennis Severs' House that functions as a "living experience museum" meant to authentically replicate life in the eighteenth and nineteenth century. In the late twentieth century, Dennis Severs restored the five-story, ten-room brick home built near Spitalfields Market, not far from the River Thames, and recreated the living conditions of an eighteenth-century middle-class silk merchant as if he were living there with his family and servants. When you walk through the doors, it is like entering the past. There is no electricity or plumbing. The house has been staged as if the family has just been called away. Beside the front entrance, in the parlor, the patriarch's great boots rest by the fire, which is real and glowing. His half-drunk glass of sherry awaits his imminent return. In the cellar, another real fire is lit, ready for the cook's fresh eggs, and there is pastry dough rolled out for baking. The smells entice you, and everything is enhanced by the warmth of the kitchen. Each floor gives you a different window into the experience of daily life in those times. I happened to attend near dusk, and as the interior became progressively darker, I felt the need for a candle even though the weak gaslighting was turned up.

In the attic, where the servants lived—and all of them slept in one bed—there was a feeble fireplace. Beside it was a small child's stool with a tiny cane, as if Tiny Tim himself had just departed. On this particular floor, the museum has unseen speakers that suddenly broadcast the faint bellows of cannon blast, as if the sound were coming off a barge floating down the nearby Thames. I learned later that the cannon was used in that way to announce important news—in this case that King William IV had just died.

There were, of course, other ways to learn about breaking news. There would have been the town crier, bellowing "Hear ye! Hear ye!" and carrying a sign with the headlines. And in later years, the newsboy would holler, "Read all about it!" as he sold his newspapers to passers-by. Nearby Hyde Park is famous for its Speakers' Corner, and on occasion people have gathered there by the thousands to hear vociferous debate. The American Revolution was fueled by debates throughout the coffeehouses and village greens of the thirteen colonies, while in the early eighteenth century, John Wesley and others who possessed great, booming, stentorian voices led the Great Awakening of evangelicals in Britain. They were able to command the attention of thousands of new converts at that time while they preached in the great outdoors.

As the industrial age fell upon the modern world, our methods of communication changed, and so too did our ability to both hear and listen to sounds in our everyday lives. When I think about the transformation of the sonic landscape, I'm reminded of a story I heard from a fellow film industry professional talking about the challenge of recreating the audio atmosphere of World War I. Gary Rydstrom, an Academy Award–winning sound designer, was working on a 2011 film adaptation of the novel *War Horse*. He wanted to create the aesthetic "sound shock" of tanks barreling through the pastoral countryside in France. The developed world was at that time experiencing a quantum leap from horses and mules to the sonic onslaught of the industrial age. The sound of the huge tanks bursting in and crushing fields and crops needed to feel too loud in the film, as it would have felt to the virgin ears of the early-twentieth-century villagers: threatening, confusing, and disorienting. Successful sound design would make the modern cinema audience experience what those people had felt. And in feeling what they felt, by hearing what they heard, they might understand them better, too.

It is impossible for us to grasp how quiet the world once was. When Alexander Graham Bell invented the telephone, people picked up the ringing line and just listened—in silence. Thus, he also had to decide on a word that could be used so the person picking up could let the caller know they were on the line; he suggested "ahoy," but it failed to catch on, and the alternative, "hello," proposed by his rival Thomas Edison, soon became widespread. Similarly, when radio communications first came in during World War I, the people on either end of a conversation soon realized that they needed to confirm they were listening—often by saying "Roger" or "Roger that" periodically. Otherwise, the speaker might worry he was talking into a silent void.

As industrialization became the driving force of modern society, the world became arguably more aggressive, overbearing, and otherworldly in its power. As we know, it also brought people by the millions out of the countryside and into the cities. In short, the gentle pace and harmony of pastoral life became a thing of the past. Another way to look at it is that the world became less kind.

Over the generations since the industrial revolution changed life as we know it, how have we tamed our noisy, cacophonous world? The government appropriates taxpayers' money to build noise barriers on highways, among other attempts to reduce noise pollution. Businesses hire sound engineers to design quieter offices, and we shelter ourselves within our own sonic silos, whether inside our cars, at home with multiple soundscapes competing for our attention (television, radio, music, and so on), or even when we are walking short distances. Staring into our screens—though they be silent—our minds are listening to what's being broadcast to us in steady, unending streams. The ubiquitous smartphone has become the great killer of small talk—the universal way we have connected since time immemorial. Equally ubiquitous today are the earbuds that cocoon us within our own private worlds. No one needs to listen to anything other than what they want to hear anymore.

In fact, we are consciously choosing to *not* listen, though the world is crying out to us to pay attention. What if we did that?

Exercise: Consciously Tune In to the World

The universe—the sun, stars, and wind—conspires to slow us down to pause, to take a breath, and in doing so, gradually we find ourselves stilled into a state of gratitude for being alive. Even just for a moment. Our ears can help us do this.

Here's a short exercise to tune in to the power of listening: Go for a walk in an urban park, along the shoreline of a beach, or stroll down a leafy street where you will undoubtedly hear the chorus of birds, or the leaves rustling. Take time for nature and tune in to your surroundings.

I often ponder the physics of all the waveforms that surround us—thinking about how sound waves travel slower than light. What we *hear* strikes us at a slower rate than what we *see*, which is instantaneous. It's my belief that when we listen—when we consciously tune in to the sounds coming to our attention—this somehow realigns our hearts and minds. We are stilled. Perhaps this is why we find ourselves in awe when we stop to look at the moon, the sunrise, or the surf rolling onto a beach.

While you're on your walk, take the time to rediscover all those sounds from the natural world seeking to grab your attention. Then note how you feel on your return. Perhaps time has somehow expanded around you. And maybe your state of mind, the people you encounter, and the rest of your day will be better for it.

**Part of doing something is listening.
We are listening. To the sun.
To the stars. To the wind.**

Madeleine L'Engle, *A Swiftly Tilting Planet*

The hidden world reveals itself when we listen.

—

Bobette Buster

2
Sound Memories

Before the invention of the phonograph in 1877, sound was considered the most ephemeral of all the senses. Sounds passed by you, like a whiff of perfume. Sound was fleeting. Uncapturable. But then Thomas Edison's phonograph cylinder played "Mary Had a Little Lamb." The world was captivated. And it was never the same again. At the end of his life, Edison, who was partially deaf, was asked which one of his over a thousand inventions was his favorite. Without hesitation he answered, "Sound recording."

Sounds has the remarkable power to evoke memories and emotional reactions at a primal level. In my work as a film consultant, I can't help but reference the quantum leap in cinema sound design since the 1970s. The directors of now-classic films including *A Clockwork Orange* (Stanley Kubrick), *A Star Is Born* (Frank Pierson), *Close Encounters of the Third Kind* (Steven Spielberg), and *The Elephant Man* (David Lynch) all sought to make sound a central part of the cinematic experience. The art form of including sound in movies had been developing since 1927, when Al Jolson first exclaimed, off the cuff, "Wait a minute, you ain't heard nothin' yet!" during *The Jazz Singer*, and from that day on, audiences the world over could not get enough of the "talkies."

But it took the cinema of the 1970s to launch the next revolution in sound—and specifically sound design. From Walter Murch's John Cage–inspired sound design for Coppola's *Godfather* trilogy to Ben Burtt's genius creation of *Star Wars* "sound characters" R2-D2, Chewbacca, *and* Darth Vadar, this era of immersive cinematic soundscapes—culminating in Walter Murch's innovative surround soundtrack for Coppola's *Apocalypse Now*—these films set the gold standard we all enjoy today.

As the technology advanced and the theater-listening experience vastly improved, sound designers were driven to experiment with how best to orchestrate emotions from sound. This could be via the long-distance whistle of a train rumbling toward you (this is always the sound of intractable destiny), a lone dog barking somewhere far off (the classic sound of loneliness), or more complex creations such as the ending of *Saving Private Ryan,* for which Rydstrom had to create the feeling of random terror. As a small band of American soldiers waits in a bombed-out French village for the dreaded arrival of the Nazis in their much-feared panzer tanks, they never actually see the tanks, but boy do they—and we—hear them. The awesome, ungodly sound of scream-like screeches from the ungreased ball bearings on the tank treads echoes off the town's walls, bringing the "monster" ever closer, louder and louder. The enemy sounds far bigger than it could be—in 3D, coming from all around them. How many of us could survive the suspense? Through sound, director Spielberg and sound designer Rydstrom capture the fear and bravery of the young men caught in life-and-death combat, and the randomness of war.

In figuring out how best to tell a story with sound, cinema sound designers ask a lot of questions. What is the story? What is the emotional subtext of this scene? What is the power that sound can bring to the viewer's overall experience of the story? How can sound best connect to the audience as they watch and listen?

Recently I have been producing a feature documentary on the power of sound and storytelling entitled *Making Waves: The Art of Cinematic Sound.* We cover many of the topics mentioned above, but we also asked each of our interviewees to name their favorite childhood sound memory. We were fortunate to interview David Lynch, who replied: "Whenever I hear the western meadowlark, it takes me right back to my grandfather's ranch, which I loved when I was a child." Walter Murch told of growing up and living within hearing distance of a clock tower in Manhattan. The clock rang out a musical motif every fifteen minutes, then rang the the respective number of tolls for each hour (one to twelve, even at midnight). He sang for us the different riffs of those quarter-hour chimes.

One of my African American colleagues, who would prefer to remain nameless, volunteered their own experience, "I can tell you my worst childhood sound memory. When I was five, I remember waking up to the sound of my parents shouting. When I looked out of my bedroom window onto our front lawn, I saw a huge burning cross, blazing bright. I learned later that it had been put there by the KKK. But what I remember most is the sound of my parents—their fear—and the crackling fire."

For me, the exercise took me back to those hot, humid summer nights at the home of my grandmother. I would be out playing with my brother, and when dusk fell, we would be called back inside. At the time, all the houses in

the small Kentucky town of Leitchfield had screen doors.
As I ran past the houses, I could hear through those screens
the televisions playing inside—the canned laughter of
a beloved sitcom or the *whack!* of a baseball bat from
a National League game and the roar of the crowd. As
the mothers called their children in, their screen doors
screeched open. And then, as we bounded inside beneath
the bright overhead fluorescent kitchen lights, the screen
doors would be left to lurch their way back to closed,
swinging, creaking, and then slamming—*thwack!* It was
the sound that we were all in now, safe and sound. By the
time I was grown up enough to leave home, everyone had
air conditioning, and those evenings of swinging screen
doors became a thing of the past. I remember missing that
most of all—that a sound of such transparency into other
people's homes, welcome realms of warm light in the dark
night, slow swinging doors seeking the latch.

Sound continued to be a touchstone to memory in my
life. My brother Charles was a classically trained singer and
ended up moving to London and becoming the lead singer
of his own pop band. He had big dreams. Sadly, both he and
his partner fell ill from AIDS and his partner passed away.
When Charles's health began to fail, I flew to London to care
for him. He died at Middlesex Hospital, aged twenty-nine, on
March 21, the first day of spring, and one of the details that
sticks with me about that day is the quiet all around me. A
heavy snow flew into the heart of London—so rare—icing
the vibrant daffodils and purple hyacinths. A caked silence
stilled the air. Something opened my ears that day. I couldn't
sleep for days, not wanting to give in to the dark, and I would
wait up for the dawn chorus of birds. It was my one delight.

Some years later, my grandmother passed on at the age of
ninety-four, and my mother and I faced the overwhelming
task of selling all her things. Her basement was filled with

all the flotsam and jetsam of nearly a century of life. Where does it all come from? There were all iterations of electronica from the 1940s onward—phones, typewriters, kitchen toasters, blenders, and several answering machines. For whatever reason—I still don't know why—I decided to plug in the last answering machine my grandmother would have used. The microcassette played out loud. It was the sound of my brother, singing with gusto from the classic Broadway musical *Oklahoma!* "Oh, what a beautiful morning! Oh, what a beautiful day! I've got a wonderful feeling everything's going my way." His laughter pealed out! He was convulsed with joy. And then he said, "Hi! I just thought I'd call to say, 'Hope you're having a good day!' I love you! Bye!" Here, in this space and time, Charles was alive. His voice was as real to me then as ever I'd known him. I was listening—in real time—to my brother. At that moment, I was given the gift of wonder. What higher power led me to turn on that one answering machine among a pile of random belongings?

Erik Aadahl, the Academy Award–nominated sound designer for *Argo* and *Transformers*, among other films, said, "If you take a picture, it's just one moment frozen in time. But if you were to freeze sound, it would just be hash. You need to be rolling on to actually hear a sound. In a sense, sound is more of a fourth dimension. It's very much tuned in to [how we] experience reality. I find that to be really profound."

Gary Rydstrom is often asked to speak before groups of all kinds, and at the end of his presentation he frequently poses this question: "If you had to choose between a photograph or an aural recording of a loved one who's passed on, which would you choose?"

I asked each documentary interviewee that very same question. As each person reflected, either a tear came to their eye or a delighted personal smile to their lips. I had the privilege of being able to pose the question to Robert Redford, who immediately said, quite matter-of-factly, "Oh, the recording. A photograph can capture a look or mood from a moment. But the voice is unique. Each person's personal possession." When I asked him if he would care to mention whom he wished he had an audio recording of, he shook his head. "No," he said, "there are too many." And he smiled.

Exercise: Create Your Own Sound Memories

Take the time to consider what major film storytellers have discovered about the power of sound to tap into our primal emotions and memories. Consider doing the following:

1. Try to remember a favorite sound memory from your childhood.

Using an audio recording device, such as your smartphone, record a voice memo and tell yourself the story of what that sound means to you now. Or, if you can record that sound—for example, birdsong, a train signal, a commercial jingle, a church bell chime—record it now. These sounds may well pass away. Upon hearing them later, you will be cast back immediately to that time and place, and it will feel "alive now."

2. Create an audio recording of a loved one.

Think about your nearest and dearest—relatives, friends, even a mentor. Again, take a few minutes to capture their laughter or speaking voice.

Also consider recording the everday chatter you hear around you. Record your children or nieces and nephews as they grow up. Just have them say a few things—you'll be very grateful to rehear their two-year-old or twelve-year-old voices and laughter much later on. Have your elders tell an anecdote or read a favorite poem aloud. Or simply capture your family hanging out, laughing, eating a meal. I have a recording made in the 1950s by my uncle, Omer Stikeleather, a captain in the air force, who brought back a large reel-to-reel recorder from his travels in Germany. Somehow, he rigged up the reel-to-reel recorder to capture my great-grandfather saying grace before dinner—a very long blessing indeed, as he called out everyone's name around the table. This audio resonates with all of us to this day. I also have a microcassette answering machine recording of my two-year-old cousin calling to ask me, in his garbled toddler language, when I'm coming to visit. But my favorite is my eighty-five-year-old great-aunt Margie (who was born in 1898), who, upon realizing that she was speaking into an answering machine, says sternly, "You know, I don't like these machines . . ." You cannot replicate these moments.

Once you have your recordings, simply label and upload these sound memories to your computer or the cloud, and maybe even add a photograph of the speaker.

3. Watch a classic film and focus on the sound design.
Francis Ford Coppola said that "sound is 50 percent of the experience" of watching a movie. The next time you want to watch a film, choose one of the iconic sound-design breakthrough films I've listed in the Resources section at the back of the book. This time, as you view the film, listen for how the sound design—not just the music—and the silence are orchestrated to make your cinematic experience far more immersive and emotionally moving.

You never really understand a person until you consider things from his point of view. . . until you climb into his skin and walk around in it.

—

Atticus Finish, *To Kill a Mockingbird*

3
When We Close Our Ears

What is it about the act of active listening that leads people to either a state of awe or total resentment: "Argh, that so-and-so made me listen for *hours* as they droned on!"

I grew up in a home where children were expected to be seen and not heard. My mother said I was a highly verbal baby and that she can't remember when I didn't talk. But around my father, I was expected to listen. He was a storyteller, a great entertainer, even an orator or polemicist who might have done exceptionally well had he entered the public arena as a politician or news commentator. Yet he became a public high school history teacher. Every night at home, fueled by Manhattan cocktails, he pontificated aloud, preparing his next-day lectures . . . and at length, brooking no interference. I learned to listen well.

Of course, I took this nightly routine for granted. For years I thought everyone listened to their father for hours on end; I only realized later on that this was not common. Most times, my father was brilliant, being well-read in current events and hilarious in his comic timing. Other times he was, well, overbearing.

Because I was seldom allowed to speak or be heard in his presence, I spoke plenty elsewhere. It wasn't until my eighty-four-year-old father knew he was dying that the table for listening finally turned toward me. He asked for me to fly to see him immediately, and when I arrived by his side, he said that I could ask him anything I wanted to. I said, "Why didn't you ever ask me about my life? Why didn't you ever let me speak?" He sighed. There was a long silence. Finally, he said, "Because I envied you. You have the life I wished I had." My conservative father had always reveled in the fact that he'd had a monthly income since the age of twenty. He was proud of his impeccable credit record. But at what cost, I thought? So I told him about the financial risks I'd had to take in my freelance career. How I'd had to learn to live way out on a limb and develop nerves of steel to endure the negotiations I'd had with major players, learning to face them eyeball to eyeball. Nothing had prepared me for that. It was trial and error. But it was an inevitable course of action if I wanted my freelance career to advance. My father stared into the long distance, and then, very quietly, he said, "You know, I could never have done that." He paused. "Thank you for telling me this." That was our last conversation. He died the following day. The silence is deafening.

Listening is a gift—one we give to ourselves and also to others. When you listen, you always get far more back than you had going into the conversation. Simply put, you know more. I know full well what it's like to live in the oxygen-deprived presence of someone who loves the sound of his own voice, and I bet many of us are familiar with the feeling of being obligated to listen to someone due to their power over us—be that a family member, a boss, or any superior. You become numb by repeated exposure.

But listening does not have to be boring. Think of it as choosing to be in tune with others. It has been said that the problem with our current social media landscape is that we are each living in our own silos, each of us in our own self-selected "filter bubbles." We only want to listen to those who are like us.

But if we choose to not listen to what makes us uncomfortable, how will we ever grow? How can a democracy exist without debate, negotiation, and compromise? Our current democratic process might appear to be broken beyond repair, but there is still much value in its ideals.

When we're not listening, we're not communicating. And a lack of communication often leads to anger and mistrust. In a 2017 *Esquire*/NBC national survey poll of three thousand adults, it was found that half were angrier than they were a year ago. People were very angry in 2016 as the presidential election revealed the gaping chasms of our fractured democracy. Political analysts and pollsters said they'd never seen anything like it. As a microcosm of the social atmosphere, I remember seeing an episode of CBS's *60 Minutes* on which a diverse group of Americans was gathered together to discuss various political issues. The protocol was that each person would take a turn responding to questions posed by the moderator, but what ended up happening was that everyone started shouting all at once. Ranting. On camera. All at the same time, with no one—not one person—giving any quarter. The commentator said there seemed to be no way to get them to stop and listen to each other before speaking.

At the beginning of the election season, before Hillary Clinton had received the Democratic Party's nomination, and before Donald Trump was even seen as a viable Republican Party candidate, David Wolpe, the Max Webb Senior Rabbi of Sinai Temple in Los Angeles, said in *Time* magazine:

> Angry people are poor communicators and even worse listeners. Their empathy is foreshortened, and they have trouble imagining the other's point of view. It makes people less healthy, and when both parties are angry, fewer are likely to find middle ground. If the only way people feel they will be heard is when they are angry, then our public discourse will be an arena for shouting past one another. Now that a sanctified modern method, a poll, has shown we're angry, perhaps we can have a reasoned public discussion about how to calm the rage and begin the work. You can be principled even when you speak in a soft voice.

And then came the results of the presidential election in November 2016. Within eight months of the first year of the forty-fifth president's four-year term, Americans witnessed white supremacists march in a tiki-torch parade while shouting Nazi slogans like "Blood and soil" on the lawn of Thomas Jefferson's beloved University of Virginia. They were protesting the removal of the statue of Confederate general Robert E. Lee. In their Unite the Right rally on August 12, 2017, tensions escalated with the arrival of counterprotesters, and more than a dozen people were injured in physical altercations. An angry male white supremacist sympathizer drove his car into the crowd, killing one of the protesters, thirty-two-year-old Heather Heyer, and injuring many others.

All of us have been forced to figure out how we got to this place. One defining factor has been the rise of social media—in particular Facebook and Twitter—whose potential dangers have been amplified by the suspicion, and very real possibility, that foreign nations may have used these channels to meddle in the democratic elections of both the United States and the United Kingdom.

As Annie Proulx, author of *Brokeback Mountain*, said in her National Book Award speech on November 16, 2017:

> This is a Kafkaesque time. . . . We observe social media's manipulation of a credulous population, a population dividing into bitter tribal cultures. We are living through a massive shift from representative democracy to something called viral direct democracy, now cascading over us in a garbage-laden tsunami of raw data. Everything is situational, seesawing between gut-response "like" or vicious confrontations. For some this is a heady time of brilliant technological innovation that is bringing us into an exciting new world. For others it is the opening of a savagely difficult book without a happy ending.

Where is the soft voice? Where is the listening? How do we find a happy ending?

———

Exercise: The Practice of Mindful Listening

Can you think of a time when someone said to you, "You're not listening to me!" How do you view that encounter now? Were you preoccupied, anxious, or angry at the time? Can you find compassion for yourself and that event now?

The next time you get into a simple argument or misunderstanding with your partner, spouse, friend, or a work colleague, just stop the discussion for a moment and do the following:

— Restate the ideas and feelings of the person who is upset. Try to do so accurately, until they are satisfied. Ask that person to do the same for you.

Sounds simple, doesn't it? Yet this will be difficult, in part because you will be stating the other person's point of view before your own. But if you practice this mindful listening process with those closest to you, it will become a known pattern. You will be creating an environment of trust. Everyone will feel heard. You will become known as someone who listens well, as opposed to a know-it-all.

Out beyond ideas of wrongdoing
and rightdoing there is a field.
I'll meet you there.
When the soul lies down in that grass,
the world is too full to talk about.

Rumi

It takes a great man to be a good listener.

—

Calvin Coolidge

4
And So It Begins

Sometimes, when things seem utterly hopeless, we hear an unlikely story. In December 2017, this story came from CNN reporters Mallory Simon and Sara Sidner.

At a courthouse in Charlottesville, Virginia, Billy Snuffer—the Imperial Wizard of the Rebel Brigade Knights (a.k.a. the Ku Klux Klan)—was there with other Klansmen. They were attending the trial of one of their colleagues charged with shooting a gun during the Unite the Right rally, the same protest where Heather Heyer was killed by the charging car.

Angry protesters shouted down the Klansmen as they attempted to enter the courthouse. Into this melee walked fifty-nine-year-old Daryl Davis, a blues musician and descendant of African slaves. As protesters screamed vitriol from the sidelines—one African American woman said, "You're a person of color; why the hell are you talking to them?" to which Davis replied, "That's right, I am a person of color, but I'm an American and so is this man right here"—Davis shook Snuffer's hand, saying, "What's going on, man, how're you doing?" The men embraced.

Daryl Davis has made it his life's work to befriend Klansmen. Many times, he is the first black person they have actually spoken to. This journey began for him when he was a ten-year-old boy facing racism in Belmont, a suburb of Boston. Even then he wondered, "How can they hate me? They don't even know me."

He began to seek out Klan members. He has been attacked and kicked. His modus operandi? He says that mostly he just listens—even as they spew hatred. He listens, thinks, and then responds, and he has been doing so for more than thirty years.

Over time, he has inspired many of these Klansmen to leave the group and, when they do, to give him their robes. At Davis's home, there are dozens of KKK robes and memorabilia hanging on his walls like museum artifacts. He does not have these things because he demanded or cajoled for them. He says they were given to him by people who had learned from him. All he did, he says modestly, was to try to reach a middle ground. He looks around at all the robes, arranging the opulent cowls and belts and, of course, the hoods, saying, "They're done. They're done. As a result of meeting me and having these conversations. Not overnight, but over time."

Walking alongside Billy Snuffer at the Charlottesville courthouse, Davis knew all too well that they made an unlikely couple. This was their second meeting. Davis was trying to find some common ground. They discussed the Klan, Nazis, and hate. Even before the CNN camera came to capture their story, Davis got Snuffer to admit that the Unite the Right rally was not about the removal of a Confederate general's statue. Davis said, "This was all about starting a race war." Snuffer agreed, "You're exactly right." As Davis listened, he was ever mindful of the KKK's history of lynching, raping, and terrorizing.

Members of the NAACP (National Association for the Advancement of Colored People) have derided Davis for associating with any member of the KKK. But Davis sees this as his life mission. Davis believes that to make change happen, "you have to find some brotherhood." At the courthouse that day, Davis appealed to the judge to consider sending the Klansman on trial to the National Museum of African American History and Culture in Washington, DC, in the way that courts mandate education for first-time offenders. Davis sat in the courtroom alongside Snuffer for two hours. His hope was that Snuffer would remember that Davis was decent that day. The Imperial Wizard witnessed a black man stand up for him against angry protesters.

When Davis got home that night, his phone rang. Billy Snuffer wanted to know if he had made it home all right. As Davis organized his room full of hanging robes given to him by Klansmen he had befriended, he reflected on his conversations with Snuffer, and the potential there was that, in listening, he might change someone's heart and mind: "And so it begins."

The story of Daryl Davis heartens me. For more than thirty years, he has taken his own free time to seek out his enemy and simply try to reach out to him, by listening. What an extraordinary thing to do. And yet, what else can we do in a democracy but agree to disagree? To try to find a way to "get on by getting along"? Surely, this is how democracies have risen to such heights of progress for the common good. I take heart in what historian and activist Howard Zinn said in his book *A People's History of the United States*: "What matters are the countless small deeds of unknown people who lay the basis of the significant events that enter history. They're the ones who have done it in the past. They're the ones who will have to do it in the future."

Listening takes time. You must pause, take a moment, and offer yourself to another person, with your full attention. Honestly, sometimes this can feel like a drag.

Maybe their issue will inconvenience you. Maybe they're confused or in emotional pain. But there will be times when listening will be the most important thing you will ever do.

Exercise: A Five-Minute Listening Practice

Can you find five minutes to give to someone—perhaps someone you know you *should* listen to more, or someone who simply needs your time and focus, even just for a few minutes? Simply listen to the other person, without judging or reacting with your eyes or sighs or any audible reactions.

See what happens . . .

Kindness is a language that the deaf can hear and the blind can see.

Mark Twain

**When people talk,
listen completely.**

—

Ernest Hemingway

5
Listen Is an Active Verb

The word "listen" contains the same letters as the word "silent."

Alfred Brendel

When you open your awareness to others, and the world, a kind of radar seems to plug in. You develop "ears to hear" in a wholly new, more alive way. Whether that's the vast array of birds calling in the great animal orchestra no matter where you live, or the frantic sounds of sirens coming from just around the corner, or the tone of your loved one's voice—their sorrow or delight—in developing ears to hear, you become more aware. It's like a kind of fine-tuning—a strengthening of your senses—no less than exercising to keep up your physical health, or learning a language or a complex art, craft, or skill to keep your brain in tip-top shape. Once you learn to tune in, you are changed forever. And you are much the better for it. Listening is an everyday act, at once ordinary and majestic. It is also an act of great generosity.

So powerful is this act that consciously choosing *not* to listen can cause great harm. It can harm not only yourself as you tune out and cut yourself off from others—sleepwalking through life and gradually losing touch with your own humanity—but also potentially cause harm to those other people, too.

Such is the tragic, true story of the murder of twenty-eight-year-old Kitty Genovese, who was walking home from her night job in the early hours of March 13, 1964. She was just at her apartment door in Queens when she was approached from behind. She was stabbed repeatedly, even as she screamed loudly for help, shouting, "Oh my God, he stabbed me! Help me!"

It was reported that many of her neighbors heard her cries for help. They closed their blinds. Someone did shout out the window, "Let that girl alone!" but to no avail. After the attacker, later identified as Winston Moseley, stabbed her, he stole forty-nine dollars from her wallet and left her on the doorstep. Kitty stumbled into the lobby but was so seriously injured, she couldn't open her locked apartment door. Still, she continued to cry for help, whereupon Moseley returned. This time, now inside the building, he stabbed her again, and then raped her before fleeing the scene. During all this, two people apparently did call the police. Then, a neighbor, Sophia Farrar, ventured out and cradled Kitty until the ambulance arrived. Kitty died on the way to the hospital. One person famously said later, "I didn't want to get involved."

In the aftermath of the crime, Kitty's neighbors and the press seemed indifferent to the event until New York City police commissioner Michael J. Murphy sought out Abe Rosenthal, the metropolitan editor of the *New York Times*, saying, "The Queens story is one for the books." Soon after, the newspaper published an investigative report, written by Martin Gansberg, with the headline "37 Who Saw Murder and Didn't Call the Police."

This event has become a standard example in social studies and psychology textbooks. The response—or nonresponse—of Kitty Genovese's neighbors is now termed the "bystander effect" or "Genovese syndrome." Over time, the story entered popular culture as a portrait of urban indifference, and it has been mythologized in television programs, books, and songs. In recent years, more analysis has revealed that the original *New York Times* report was flawed; in particular the number of "witnesses" was found to be a gross exaggeration. And yet the bystander effect is still a force in human interaction. As professor Harold Takooshian wrote in 2014 in *Psychology Today*, "When Chief of Detectives Albert Seedman asked him [Winston Moseley] how he dared to attack a woman in front of so many witnesses, the psychopath calmly replied, 'I knew they wouldn't do anything; people never do.'" Moseley confessed to not only Kitty's murder but to two other fatal attacks nearby.

The witnesses' lack of response is attributed to what psychologists call *diffusion of responsibility*, a socio-psychological phenomenon when people in groups of three or more are less likely to act responsibly. This phenomenon has also been used to explain the behavior of European citizens who failed to act during the countless World War II atrocities carried out by the Nazis.

When you listen to a witness,
you become a witness.

Elie Wiesel

Listening can become a responsibility—a call to action to save another person's life, a revelation of humanity. And that's when listening reveals character. Throughout history, we have stories of individuals who listened and responded to the call to action, no matter their own personal pain and loss, and we remember and honor them to this day.

Learning to listen means you're becoming mature, a true adult. You may well discover your life's purpose. You will experience what it is to become fully alive. But over time, this one thing has proven to be equally true: denying what you hear—cutting off the call to action—will inexorably lead to a person becoming lost to themselves forever.

———

My mandate going into the Weinstein story was never to *believe* all survivors; it was to *listen* to all survivors. I think it's completely possible to be both a sceptical, judicious reporter and also create a space for survivors to be heard. If that reporting inspires people to activism, then it's a job done well.

Ronan Farrow, *The Hollywood Reporter*, January 10, 2018

On October 5, 2017, the *New York Times* published an investigative report by Jodi Kantor and Megan Twohey about Hollywood mogul Harvey Weinstein's sexual harassment pattern—his widely known abuse of power and the complicity machine that surrounded him. A few days later, the first of reporter Ronan Farrow's in-depth articles gave his well-known victims more time to speak. These stories rocked Hollywood and led to an industry-wide reckoning. Within just three months, the silence was shattered in a way it hadn't been before, with the #MeToo movement, which inspired women to come forward and expose via social media the powerful men who had sexually harassed them. Farrow's article in the *New Yorker* on November 6, 2017, led to the unparalleled downfall of Weinstein. At the time of this writing he is under criminal investigation, his wife has left him, and his company has collapsed. Still more #MeToo stories from high-profile women continue to spill out about other industry titans.

A cascade of public firings has ensued. Women are marching. We are now witnessing a major cultural shift, led by the idea of listening.

Most of the men outed by their accusers denied any wrongdoing. Some said they had been misrepresented, that it was a case of consensual sex and now they were experiencing "political hit jobs" (a term coined by former Fox News star Bill O'Reilly). Some acknowledged the pain they caused, but without really apologizing to their victims.

But Louis CK, a prominent comedian, came out immediately with a fresh new take. He responded to his six accusers, saying, "These stories are true." People were surprised by his frankness. He acknowledged his abuse of power and how perverse and one-sided his perspective was. Then, he concluded his statement with, "I have spent my long and lucky career talking and saying anything I want. I will now step back and take a long time to listen." The last word, finally. *Listen.*

The #MeToo movement has swept the entertainment and media industry, taking down even its lasting icons. Charlie Rose was an anchor of *CBS This Morning* and the host and producer of the PBS show *Charlie Rose* since 1991. The seventy-six-year-old could talk to anyone and was considered the embodiment of the gracious conversationalist who made everyone—especially his audiences—feel welcome at his round oak table. Using the same #MeToo hashtag, a number of women reported a pattern of sexual advances by Rose when they were young interns or employees invited to his elegant estate, and CBS News immediately fired Rose, and PBS canceled his show.

The takedown of such a high-profile and widely respected personality would have been unheard of even just a year ago. Social media had a newfound purpose and cause. With #MeToo, women would no longer be silenced.

The day after Rose's firing, his CBS cohost, Gayle King, was asked to appear on the station's *Late Show with Steven Colbert*. There was a very sensitive moment between King and Colbert on camera.

Colbert has been a long-standing comedic foil and he easily stepped into the role of highlighting the follies and foibles of the many powerful men who abused their positions by harassing women. He was equally merciless to Charlie Rose, especially when it came to Rose's age and the very young women he continually seemed to hire to work on his PBS show. Gayle King was not pleased at the laughter Colbert was garnering at Rose's expense. Colbert said, "What is it that you think we men should now do?" She said she was angry and numb and didn't know how to answer. She seemed genuinely flummoxed. But then she acknowledged, "Well, even though Charlie Rose was my friend, and I have always admired him, I cannot stop thinking about those young women. He does not get a pass on this one. It's time women are believed. We really need to know that men come into the conversation or nothing can change."

Colbert: "Well, what's the best way for men to join the conversation other than listen and believe?'

King: "To listen and say it's not going to be tolerated."

Suddenly, listening has become a very important part of the conversation when it comes to power politics. The implication is that when you listen, your heart becomes open to change. You see the world from a perspective other than your own.

When I was growing up, it seemed as if every classic Western featured the line "You can never truly understand a man until you've walked a mile in his moccasins." The point is to understand a person before judging them. This very sentiment became a theme of the civil rights movement in the 1960s, and it is equally relevant to the worldwide #MeToo movement.

On February 9, 2018, *Quartz*, a sister publication of *The Atlantic*, published the first in a four-part series on gender equality. "The Visionaries" featured interviews with "50 of the world's most qualified and ambitious women across every industry about how they achieved their success . . . from Sheryl Sandberg and Tarana Burke to Emily Weiss and Zhang Xin." When the women in the series were asked what they wanted from men, the resounding answer was, "Just listen to us."

Perhaps this presages a new era of civility.

It takes two to speak the truth,
one to speak, and another to hear.

—

Henry David Thoreau

6
Listening Brings Truth

"Listen to your life as it whispers to you." Oprah Winfrey often speaks of this, her abiding life principle. She says, "In all my years of doing *The Oprah Show*, I wanted to say it a thousand times. My staff counted, and told me I'd said it only thirty-three times. But I was thinking it all the time." How often do we listen to ourselves? That small voice that, perhaps, speaks the truth. And if we did, what might we learn? Where might it lead us?

We know Oprah as a self-made billionaire and leading cultural force, but to fully understand her success, it is worth looking at her formative early years. She talks freely about her young life: how she was raised by her grandmother in poor, rural Mississippi; the shame she endured as an unwed pregnant teenager whose baby died shortly after birth; her longing to be an actress; and her strivings to fit in as a television reporter—in spite of her TV news boss saying she was "too too," meaning she put "too much" of herself into the story, on camera, to be a professional reporter. To fill out the last months of her contract, he eventually gave her an afternoon talk show in Baltimore, and it was then that she had a major breakthrough. She desperately wanted to act in the 1985 film *The Color Purple*, believing that Alice Walker's novel was really *her* story. When a casting director came to Chicago, Oprah was able to audition for the role of Sofia. But after the audition, she heard nothing. Finally, she called the casting director's office in Hollywood. He told her in no uncertain terms that she had no business calling him. He said he was in the process of auditioning a very experienced, well-known actress for the role, because, as she well knew, Steven Spielberg would be directing the film. Crestfallen, Oprah went away to a weight-loss camp, a "fat farm," as she called it.

While out jogging, she listened to *that* whisper, deep inside her, but she also knew that she had to let go of her deep desires if she wanted to be happy. She would bless the actress who would get the job. It was all she could do to "let go." As she tells the story, she said she began to sing the gospel song "I Surrender All." And then suddenly she heard a voice shouting from outside the weight-loss facility. There was an important call for her in the main office. Oprah raced inside to find Steven Spielberg on the phone. He told her that he had chosen her for Sofia. Then he added that he didn't want her to lose any weight for the role. Overjoyed, Oprah drove home that day and stopped by Dairy Queen to enjoy her favorite ice cream treat to celebrate. To this day, she says, she starts each day by listening, meditating, taking time apart.

In her book, *Beyond the Label: Women, Leadership, and Success on Our Own Terms*, Maureen Chiquet, former global CEO of Chanel, speaks about the unlikely trajectory of her successful rise in retail from Gap to Old Navy to Chanel—or, as she puts it, from "mass to class"—because she learned how to listen.

Mickey Drexler, then CEO of Gap, was Chiquet's dynamic boss. She says that "Mickey Meetings" were the stuff of lore, their purpose being to attain his approval and sign-off on final product assortments and buying plans for the next season. There was a reason that Wall Street called Drexler the "merchant prince": he had a near-perfect batting average at picking bestsellers. In one meeting in particular, Chiquet wanted to show that she was not afraid to take risks and was eager to reveal her "new secret weapon—a fantastic new fabric in a trendy new fit." But during the meeting Drexler's passionate, volatile ripostes only made her defend her choices harder. Finally, he told her that he couldn't stand there and argue with her anymore—she wasn't listening. And with that, he stormed out of the meeting. When she got back to her office, Drexler called her. She braced herself. Was she about to be fired? Instead, he told her she had potential, good taste, and the eye for bestsellers. But, he told her, she had to learn to listen. "I am just asking you to stop, open your ears, and hear what people have to say. If you don't, you'll never be a great merchant. . . . You need to listen better."

When he hung up, Chiquet realized what a big lesson she had just been given by the CEO of one of the most successful retail companies in America. Chiquet writes: "He cared enough to teach me one of the most important lessons I would ever learn. To listen. To listen deeply." In that moment, Chiquet realized that if she wanted to succeed in business and in life she would have to practice listening.

Chiquet went on to become one of the top merchants at Gap and was then given the opportunity to build Old Navy as a great new brand in mass consumer retail. As her star rose, management asked her to complete an assessment to review any gaps in her leadership. She would be soliciting feedback from the people around her: direct reports, peers, and bosses. The assessment came back overall very favorable. One detail that emerged, however, was that her colleagues loved to learn from her but also suggested that she ask them their opinions and take time to consider where they were coming from. The woman who was sharing the results of the assessment with Maureen told her, "I want you to appreciate what you do well, but this is about seeing yourself from another's perspective."

What tough medicine, but great wisdom: to dare to see ourselves as others see us. Most of us wouldn't want to know. But as the late, great Scottish poet Robert Burns wrote, "O wad some Power the giftie gie us To see oursels as ithers see us," or, in modern English, "O, would that some Power give us the gift of seeing ourselves as others see us!"

Chiquet took this assessment to heart. She changed her approach. Soon, armed with her new leadership skills, she was named president of Banana Republic. Around this time, Chiquet was also being courted by major headhunters; all she knew about it was that a top luxury brand was looking for a new global CEO. She took various meetings over a couple of years but thought no more about it until she was offered the opportunity to become the global CEO for Chanel, Inc. The transition came with this caveat: she had to spend three full years of training before taking on complete responsibility. In particular, she was asked to do nothing but listen. For an entire year. This would allow her to garner intelligence from the company's highly seasoned and tenured employees and develop an appreciation of and respect for the creative process.

"My willingness to let go of my need to prove myself and embrace this silent period as an opportunity to learn (albeit frustrating at times) helped me earn the trust of my new team members whose experience and expertise were much deeper than mine. . . . It required patience and humility," said Chiquet. She could see that taking leadership would not be about espousing a grand vision or waving a flag, but that she had to ask a lot of questions. And as she listened to their answers, she would "listen for what tensions and concern lay just under the surface." It was a type of curiosity that became contagious. Her team began to ask more focused questions. Finally, she realized that, as a company, they would have to listen much more to their customers, their employees, and the world around them.

When Chiquet was free to lead Chanel into a whole new era—combining her expertise in online retail, social media, and appealing to a new generation of mass consumers with the mystique of Chanel's couture-class appeal—she had an aha moment. She had gone too far in the wrong direction. "I was listening too much to everyone else and, as a consequence, I [was] left feeling unanchored from the vision and values I knew we needed to forge ahead. My team could see it, too . . . I'd been so focused on empathizing with others that I risked losing my way as their leader." This seemed to be an all too common complaint of women leaders, and Chiquet knew it.

She then found her way to a rather unorthodox coach: horse whisperer Koelle Simpson, based in California. In the theory of horse-human relationships, it is said that the horse mirrors the human. They take their cues from us, and reflect back who we are. They either follow you or they don't. (See the documentary film *Buck*, directed by Cindy Meehl, for the true story of the man who inspired Robert Redford's *The Horse Whisperer*.) Through her work with Simpson, Chiquet was able to look at herself through a new lens, and she came home to the truth of who she really was. And she believed in herself as a leader.

Chiquet returned to Chanel, now more confident and fully integrated in both sides of the values of listening, she was able to say, "Real authority comes when you are able to strike the right balance. You need to listen to others, and you need to be attuned to yourself."

She went on to lead Chanel through major market disruptions, upheavals, and creative innovations. Today, the company thrives as the top luxury brand for the twenty-first century across all retail platforms—a feat very few luxury brands have been able to achieve, let alone expand upon or even maintain. In 2016, Chiquet decided to leave Chanel, proud of what she had accomplished, and not sure what her next adventure will be. But one thing she knew was that she had to listen to her inner voice and be true to herself.

Deep Listening

Both Oprah and Chiquet have attained that all-too-rare pinnacle for women today: they became leaders whose influence transformed their chosen fields. They achieved this by applying the principles of "deep listening."

As Oprah said in her Harvard University commencement address in 2013: "I have to say that the single most important lesson I learned in twenty-five years talking every single day to people was that there is a common denominator. We want to be validated. We want to be understood. After thirty-five thousand interviews, as soon as the camera shut off, everyone turned to me and inevitably asked, 'Was that okay?' I heard from President Bush, President Obama, even Beyoncé. Friends and family, your enemies, strangers in every encounter, in every exchange, they want to know this one thing: Was that okay? Did you hear me? Did what I say mean anything to you?"

As she ended her historic Harvard address she said, "But I know this: if you're willing to listen to, be guided by, that inner voice that is the GPS within yourself, to find out what makes you come alive, you will be more than okay. You will be happy, you will be successful, and you will make a difference in the world."

She concluded: "Thank you for listening. Was that okay?"

A key part of deep listening is the courage and the willingness to see ourselves as others see us—which can be both mortifying and deeply gratifying—and then to still listen to the truth of who we really are. Listening always leads us to this wisdom: be true to who you really are.

I have been a seeker and I still am. But I stopped asking the books and the stars. I started listening to the teaching of my soul.

Rumi

Exercise: Deep Listening in Five Minutes

What if you set aside five minutes—alone—to just listen to yourself?

Make this *your* time. Switch off or set aside any distractions—phone, computer, TV, and so on. You may say you're too busy, but perhaps you can incorporate this exercise into something you're already doing. For example, see if you can give yourself five extra minutes to sit in the car before you head in to work or before you pick up your children.

Ideally you want to find a safe, quiet space. If not the car, this could be a favorite armchair, a park bench, or—again—go on a short walk. Try to take yourself away from the normal hustle and bustle.

Look up and around. Find *one beautiful thing* to focus on—the sky, clouds, a tree—then:

— Pause. Just listen. You will hear a rattling of thoughts, lists, worries—this is what meditation gurus call your "monkey mind."

— Allow your monkey mind to flow past you for a minute or two. (Think of this as "white noise," or the irritating sound of a lawnmower or faraway hum you can't control.) Ignore it all.

— Only. Listen. To. Yourself.

— Breathe in for seven beats. Breathe out for eleven beats. Repeat for one minute.

— Focus on your breath. If your mind drifts, choose just one word—make it a positive word—to guide you back to your breath. If you are afraid, anxious, or angry, feel free to shout or scream (yes, that's allowed!). Just let it all out.

— Then breathe. And listen.

This will be difficult at first. You will become easily distracted or bored. But if you can give yourself five minutes a day for 180 days, this practice *will* change your life. Like strengthening a muscle, see if you can work up to twenty minutes, interspersed throughout the day. Create a pattern. This is an intention—a promise to yourself.

After time and practice, you can expect your "monkey mind" to filter down. All the irritating thoughts will settle like silt in a rushing river until the water clears and you can see everything. You will have clarity. And you will— at last—hear the "still, small voice" of your deep inner wisdom that's been whispering to you all along.

Listening happens in time. Take the time to come apart from the noise and distractions, and welcome what you might be able to hear in the silence.

And what happened next?

—

Bobette Buster

7

How We Learn to Listen Differently

> If a man does not keep pace with his companions, perhaps it is because he hears a different drummer. Let him step to the music which he hears, however measured or far away.

Henry David Thoreau

Listening is the foundation for respect, for the right of the other person to be different. In my case, it wasn't a person who taught me this lesson. It was my dog. Luna is a very beautiful, smart tri-color Shetland sheepdog, also known as a Sheltie. When she took over my life as a four-month-old puppy, I was completely unprepared and overwhelmed. My parents had never allowed us to have pets. They had grown up on farms full of animals—cows, pigs, horses, and, yes, cats and dogs— yet their philosophy was that animals should never be domesticated; they belonged on farms where they could roam free. Nevertheless, my three brothers and I each got ourselves a dog and a cat when we left home.

But I was completely flummoxed by the demands of this little puppy. Why couldn't she behave like my cat? Be independent, take care of her own business, walk thin, sit fat. Instead Luna spoke to me—at length—in a wild and foreign language of yelps, pips, growls, and barks. A herding animal, she was always attempting to get me to do something I didn't understand. I didn't know how to respond. I kept thinking that I needed to behave like the alpha in the pack; then she would follow my lead. But no, there was some other communication bandwidth we would have to find together if we were ever to have a happy home. For one, I hadn't realized what a responsibility it was to have to walk her three, even four times a day! Cats didn't need this kind of attention . . . Plus, Luna didn't really walk. Rather, she dawdled, taking her sweet time to smell every single new daily *drop of information* left by her fellow dogs. This also meant that I had to speak to strangers, or rather fellow dog lovers, whose dogs always wanted to play with Luna. On a regular basis I was impatient, bored even, until I began to notice that they were amused by her cute, playful romping.

Then one day, while we were out on the street, she stopped, sat bolt upright, and then began to howl. Across the crowded street—literally full of dogs of every breed imaginable—Luna spied the only male Sheltie in the neighborhood, the very handsome Robbie, I was soon to learn. Robbie raced across the street, his owner, M'Leigh, in tow. For Robbie and Luna, it was kismet. They leaped high in the air, bumped their chests, and chewed each other's ears while circling round and round. In short, it was love at first sight. Thereafter, Luna pawed and chirped at me in a very special way every single day whenever she sensed that Robbie was nearby. And she was always right! I began to learn the language of Luna. Dog-behavior scientists say that shepherd dogs, as a breed, can learn up to one thousand words or commands in our language. But, equally so, I learned how to tune in to her specific barks. I learned the difference between her whimper when she was thirsty and her whine to go outside, and her sneezes of delight when a favorite friend came to visit. As I opened up to her, she encouraged me to slow down and take the time to walk, look, and listen. Before long a new world had opened up to me: the dawn chorus of Southern California, the whoosh of the ravens and the wild parrots cawing throughout the day, and, in the night, the raucous, howling coyotes. As I tuned into her worldview, I perceived her extra-sensory awareness of danger—far-off sirens or an approaching skateboarder—or of promise—as with the heady sound of a plastic bag being ever-so-quietly pulled open in a room on the other side of the house: a dog treat, for sure, beckoned. She would bound in, her fluffy white tail waving high at full mast. My world expanded when I accepted our differences. She became a very happy, well-adjusted dog. And I met my neighbors.

Listening can feel like walking into a vast park. It creates a wide open space to find common ground among strangers. There is no other way but by and through *listening* that we can find similarities. While you are crossing the barrier of your own ego by listening to another's point of view, you are also creating an opening in order to find a new way forward—a new hope in the world.

History continually reveals that revolutions—whether violent or peaceful—take place when someone speaks truth into the age in such a way that people can "develop an imagination" to embrace a wholly new worldview. One such person was Muhammad Ali. He ushered in a phenomenal era of American sportsmanship in the 1960s that also coincided with the efforts toward racial equality as put forth in the civil rights movement. Muhammad Ali's birth name was Cassius Clay, after the highly revered albeit eccentric nineteenth-century abolitionist. The Clay who would become Muhammad Ali rose up out of total obscurity, hailing from a poor neighborhood in Louisville, Kentucky, and then bursting onto the world scene at the age of sixteen with extraordinary bravado, self-confidence, and boxing talent. The young Cassius Clay won an Olympic gold medal in Rome in 1960, and one year later, he became a professional heavyweight boxer. At age twenty-two, he won the heavyweight championship of the world. He shouted over and over, "I AM THE GREATEST!" Clay intuitively understood the power of PR, and he charmed the world with his quotable poetry, memorably explaining his pugilistic tactics with the line "I'm going to float like a butterfly and sting like a bee." A year later, Clay converted to Islam and changed his name to Muhammad Ali.

As his star rose, Ali believed he could change the world's view of his skin color. He would go on a television show and then interrupt the interviewer by saying, "Ain't I pretty? Tell everyone I'm pretty." While everyone laughed, the interviewer would agree that, yes, Ali was quite good-looking. Ali's charm offensive was masterful: African Americans had always been judged by their appearance—now Ali was asking to be praised for how he looked. He was as fast a wit in an interview as he was in the ring.

From the time of Ali's arrival on the scene in the 1960s, everyone was astounded by how masterfully he took to the world stage. *And they listened.* He was admired by the press—and not just the sports broadcasters—and often quoted. They were bowled over by his self-possession, his power of presentation.

During his sports reign, the sheer audacity of how Muhammad Ali carried himself mesmerized a young boy from Long Island. Billy Crystal, a short white Jewish guy, adored Ali, the tall, commanding African American from the South. Crystal studied Ali for hours to understand his voice, his inflections, and his cadence—he listened carefully to how Ali spoke his truth.

Crystal was especially taken with the great duo of Ali and legendary sports commentator Howard Cosell. The two powerhouses were famous for their verbal jousting in interviews, and Crystal deeply admired how they both reshaped America's view of diversity, class, and race—just by being great showmen. Crystal began to perform a "duet skit" impersonating Cosell and Ali in comedy clubs around New York City, and the act in turn uplifted Cosell's interviews with Muhammad Ali; as a kind of counterpunch, further setting up Ali's comedic persona. Crystal's act remains today a masterpiece of the high art of interpretation—going far beyond comedy or impersonation.

Then, one day in 1974, Billy was asked to be the keynote speaker at a major event honoring Ali. It was make-or-break time for Crystal, who was nervous as hell. His mimicry was entirely based on how well he had listened to—and internalized the truth of—who Ali was as a man. And Crystal understood Ali, with a mysterious kind of depth and appreciation for how Ali was transforming America. When Crystal came on, Ali couldn't believe what he was hearing. Crystal commanded the evening. He brought down the house, as they say, and he did it not just with sidesplitting laughter but with a wave of astonishment and awe. Ali called him over and said, "You're my brother now. My little brother." The men remained close friends until Ali's death in 2016.

When Ali died at the age of seventy-four, the nation mourned. His funeral was broadcast live. Former president Bill Clinton spoke, and President Barack Obama sent a video with his condolences. For more than three hours, world leaders in politics, charity, sports, and the Muslim world extolled Ali's impact and achievements.

Billy Crystal was the second-to-last speaker at the funeral. It would be Crystal's last great impersonation of Ali. Crystal peppered his moving eulogy with perfectly executed imitations of the late Ali. After years of careful listening, Crystal was in tune with who Muhammed Ali was as both a man and a legend; Crystal had perfected the dance of listening. His ability to precisely and truthfully convey Ali demonstrates the power of true listening: when we tune into others' stories and internalize their truths, we see them for who they really are and they teach us to see the world in a new way.

Exercise: Who Do You Listen To?

We are, all of us, always listening to someone who is influencing our life—for good or bad. Use the following exercise to better understand the figures that impact your life.

1. Reflect on who have you been listening to. Who has influenced you in ways you've never consciously acknowledged? Think about rock stars, sports stars, cultural leaders, poets, performers, politicians, preachers. Maybe you've listened to some bad influencers, or people you've now outgrown; perhaps you can now perceive their influence with new eyes and ears.

2. Who made you see the world differently and influenced or even changed you? Do you still listen to that person? Do you hand off their thoughts or worldview to others you encounter? Is this what you *want* to do?

3. Who would you listen to now if you could? Revisit some classic recordings: the speeches of Martin Luther King Jr., Gandhi, and Winston Churchill; interviews with Mother Teresa; Marian Anderson singing at the foot of the Abraham Lincoln Memorial; J. K. Rowling reading *Harry Potter* . . . there are so many. See the Resources section at the back of the book for details on where to find some.

Take your time. Listen to how, from the timbre of their voice, these people are teaching you something new even today. When we hear recordings from the past, they become alive again, strike us anew, and provide our hearts and minds with fresh insight.

Listening only happens with time.
Take the time.
Your life will expand.

—

Bobette Buster

8

The Foundation for Respect

A viral Facebook thread I saw recently posed the following question: "Is it possible that an idea is valid if you don't agree with it?" The post went on to ask, "Can you think of a time recently when—even if you didn't agree with the other person—you realized that their position was just as valid as yours, you just didn't agree with it?"

There then ensued a very long thread in which some commentors said that it was impossible to accept an idea as valid if you didn't agree with it, while others equivocated, saying that maybe it was possible, but it hadn't happened to them. A few said that Facebook was no forum for real discourse. And, as is now all too common, a few snarky remarks were left, too. Still, the question generated a lot of discussion from all angles.

When I think about the clash between strongly opposed viewpoints, I'm reminded of the TV show *All in the Family*, created by one of the great American television producers, Norman Lear. The series ran from 1971 to 1979, at a time when the country was perhaps far more polarized than it is even today. Lear created the series during the Vietnam War culture crisis, and the cast of characters featured the now infamous outspoken blue-collar arch-conservative Archie Bunker, played by Carroll O'Connor, who was set up in opposition to his shaggy-haired, denim-wearing, liberal son-in-law, Meathead, played by Rob Reiner. In every episode, Archie gets ramped up into a terrible row with his son-in-law and/or his long-suffering wife, Edith (played by Jean Stapleton), until he shouts, "Stifle yourself!" Of course, we, the audience are able to see the real story as we watch this unashamed racist, sexist man struggle with the way the world was changing. In perhaps the most iconic episode, Meathead finds himself, yet again, trying to knock some sense into Archie. But Archie blocks his every comment by singing "God Bless America" until everyone leaves the room. Archie gleefully finishes the entire anthem. Alone.

This episode is the embodiment of what happens when we don't listen, when we don't look for common ground to find a new way forward. We shout each other down with our own righteous indignation. But what good comes from singing alone?

Norman Lear once said, "This is the most emotionally cluttered era in history." That was true back then, and some might say it's even more cluttered now. We are facing true challenges to our country, to our democracy, and to the values that many of us hold dear, such as freedom of the press and the right to protect our election process. The very idea of "Truth" is being challenged. So how can we listen with confidence? What if we are being manipulated and fed lies? How can we cut through the clutter? How do we move toward a culture of civility and dignity?

In the 2016 presidential election, the pollsters and news media could not get a grip on the severe polarization that divided America. Each side was often seen shouting at the other. But a new kind of activism was developing.

Ordinary citizens were going door to door to find common ground among those in the opposition. They held open forums of conversation. In seven states and the District of Columbia, female restaurant workers—both Republicans and Democrats—organized themselves to support the One Fair Wage campaign to bring an end to taking their wages from shared tips. When women on the Democratic side approached their Republican counterparts, they simply said, "Can we agree that we all need one fair wage for all?" Yes, they replied. Consensus was achieved on that one shared concern. This was hailed as a new starting ground in the campaign for a raise in the minimum wage for both male and female low-income restaurant workers. All would now share the same wage.

In January 2018, the government shut down. The Republicans, who controlled both the House and Senate, and the Democrats could not agree on a new budget to keep the government open. But finally, two dozen centrist senators from both sides gathered in the office of Senator Susan Collins (R-Maine) to find common cause, with the help of a Masai tribal talking stick. The stick was a gift from Senator Heidi Heitkamp (D-North Dakota). Collins's talking stick procedure had simple ground rules: anyone who wished to voice an opinion could speak only once they took hold of the talking stick. There were rumors that the stick was not always used as intended (one rumor said it was once thrown across Collins's office), and outside in the halls and meeting rooms of Congress both sides were still blaming the other for the shutdown. Collins's group, which had named itself the Common Sense Coalition, persisted in their negotiations, however, and within three days they found consensus and the government was reopened.

Voicing everyone's surprise, Senator Joe Manchin (D-West Virginia) exclaimed, "We have basically taken over

Susan's office as our little Switzerland. That's where we meet in a bipartisan way. Everyone talks with each other, trying to help each other, and not at each other."

The talking stick is not a new concept. Also called a "speaker's staff," it is used by the indigenous tribes of the Pacific Northwest. The stick is passed around a group, from member to member, and it allows everyone to be heard. It gives the more introverted members time to speak, while also keeping long-winded individuals from dominating the discussion.

But what do you do if you do your part to listen and still can't find common ground with someone, or find yourself utterly opposed? How do we get to the other side of a stalemate or standoff?

I had an experience in Israel a few years ago with a young taxi driver that has stayed with me. I've often wondered if I did the right thing.

I had been touring Jerusalem and was finally taking a cab to Tel Aviv's Ben Gurion Airport to fly home to the United States. The taxi driver picked me up at the hotel for the hour-long drive. How many times have I been in a cab with an unknown driver? I didn't think of this driver as any different from the hundreds I'd had before. The man who picked me up was probably in his twenties, and he spoke fluent English. As we had a long ride to the airport, I asked him a bit about his life. He said he was Palestinian, and so I asked him how it was for him living in Israel these days. For some reason, he then decided to take this opportunity to vent his rage about how the United States had announced the death of Osama bin Laden. He said he didn't believe that the United States actually found and killed bin Laden, that it was all a story, like a Hollywood script the U.S. government had made up in order to deceive their enemies. After all, there was no picture of his body. I interjected then, saying, "Well, it was felt that showing photos of the body would be seen as a desecration of Islamic burial laws." My comment, meant to be helpful, only incensed him further. He began to get even more angry, saying that the United States was a great, tyrannical evil, and that by announcing that Osama bin Laden was dead, we were just trying to brainwash the world and to, in particular, threaten the Muslim world. I tried to speak softly so as to calm his ire: "In spite of what you may have heard in the media, we welcome Muslims from all over the world." But he retorted that this was just another lie. I was in the back seat of his cab. There was no place for me to go. He was becoming increasingly angry. But what I was acutely aware of was that he knew that I, as an American woman, was listening to him. And all I could hope for at that moment was that I offered him the sense that he was being heard.

While he ranted, I thought to myself that I couldn't say for certain that Osama bin Laden had been found and killed by Navy SEALs. I said to myself, "Well, yes, I took it on good faith that the U.S. government did that. I believed President Obama was telling the truth when he announced Osama bin Laden's death on television." But what would I gain by restating what he already knew I believed? None of us had seen the body, so we couldn't really know. I accepted that the U.S. government had done it, and he did not. So all I could do was listen to this very angry person, infuriated by the imperial hegemony of the United States. I felt that he was the kind of young man who needed to be persuaded that we were not all evil, but I felt the best way to do that was not by talking but by listening.

And so all I did was *listen*. I hoped he would notice that I wasn't arguing with him. I wasn't saying, "You're wrong." I looked him in the eye as he was looking at me through the rearview mirror. I hoped that showing him these small decencies would count for something. When we finally got to the airport, he quietly and courteously pulled out my luggage and sat it on the curb. He stared straight at me and thanked me.

Out of respect for his culture, I knew that as a woman I should not shake his hand, and so I bowed my head and then paid and tipped him. Then I said, "Thank you for the ride. I wish you well." There was the briefest hint that he was a bit ashamed that he had ranted at me for a full hour, but I felt it was far more important that he could feel the sense that he had been heard—whether I agreed with him or not. Maybe that counted for something.

My hope was that by my being open to listening to him on that one-hour journey, perhaps a crack would appear in the solid wall of his opinion. As Leonard Cohen sang, "There is a crack in everything. That's how the light gets in."

Exercise: Listening Requires Courage

Eminent psychologist Carl Rogers said, "If you really understand another person . . . without any attempt to make evaluative judgments, you run the risk of being changed yourself. [For] the great majority of us . . . listening would seem too dangerous. So the first requirement is courage."

We all have someone in our lives with whom we think we can never find accord. We cannot bear to listen to them, or expect them to ever listen to us. But what if we could find a new way? Would you dare to do this one new good thing? What would it take for you to try to create a new path of understanding?

For those seemingly impossible impasses—marital breakdown, troublesome teenagers, neighbor or family disputes—consider following these ten steps:

1. Change the setting.
Take yourselves apart from the usual hustle and bustle of life. Seek comfort and beauty. Instead of sitting on opposite sides of a table—as if in a divorce lawyer's conference room—find a warm, welcoming setting and seat yourselves in comfortable chairs, perhaps facing a beautiful view. You should be able to see each other but also free to let your eyes settle on a longer view. Attendees of the conflict-resolution program known as the Oxford Process (many of whom are from the most anguished, wartorn regions of the world) are taken on a retreat, housed in beautiful Cotswold cottages, and served elegant food, the idea being that comfortable circumstances will help facilitate discussion.

2. Treat each other courteously.
Offer the other person a seat and a cup of tea or coffee. Pour it out for them. Ask about their well-being. Are they comfortable? What else can you do for them?

3. Seek common ground.
To neutralize intense feelings, start by discussing something shared and ordinary: the weather, traffic, what movies or major sports events have happened lately. No politics!

4. Make sure both sides are allowed to speak, and be listened to, for an equal amount of time.
Listen fully to each other, with no interruptions or interjections. No righteous indignation, no visual or audible cues of disapproval, no list making or writing anything down.

5. Paraphrase what you've heard.

Once the first person has finished speaking, the other person should paraphrase what they heard. Perhaps an insight has already been gained. "Oh, I never thought about that!" "Oh, really, how was that?" Seek understanding.

6. Take turns.

Now the other person gets the chance to speak for the same amount of time. And then the first person will paraphrase what they heard and understood. If the listener's paraphrase does not reflect what the speaker was trying to say, the speaker can rephrase using different words and allow the listener to paraphrase again.

7. Try to understand, not judge.

Both sides are free to speak their truth and their pain. To tell their side of the story. Express your feelings. Dredge up the roots of your bitterness. Expose the wounds. Now is the time.

By paraphrasing, the listening party must then reflect back how you felt, the hope being that they will begin to get a sense of how it might have felt had they gone through those things. Carl Rogers has said that "defensive distortions drop away with astonishing speed as people find the only intent of this experience is to understand, not to judge."

8. Involve a third party if necessary.

In certain cases you may need to include a third party. Their role will be to reflect each person's position to the other party. We can more easily understand the feelings of another person when their attitude is accurately described to us by a third party.

9. Expect there to be an aha moment (even if it's just a small one).
Remember: once you have seen the world the way the other person sees it—without passing any judgment—*you run the risk of being changed yourself.* This may well change your entire world—not to mention that it could upset others around you. But this is the beginning of a more understanding society.

10. Discover humility or ask for forgiveness.
Dare to let go of the past and find a new way forward.

We can all endeavor to practice this process of learning to listen well and daring to understand each other. Perhaps the real story behind these difficult times is that we are entering a new era. Some are already calling it the Age of Empathy.

Listening only happens with time. Take the time. Your life will expand.

—

Bobette Buster

9
Listen, Really Listen

Ring out, wild bells, to the wild sky . . .

Ring out the old, ring in the new . . .
Ring out the false, ring in the true . . .

Ring out the want, the care, the sin,
The faithless coldness of the times . . .

Ring out false pride in place and blood,
The civic slander and the spite;
Ring in the love of truth and right,
Ring in the common love of good.

Alfred, Lord Tennyson, *In Memoriam CVI*

When I was a student at Northwestern University, near
Chicago, I was extremely fortunate to study under the
groundbreaking professor of speech and performance
arts Charlotte I. Lee, whose mantra was, "Listen, *really
listen* to the words." She taught us to apply the concept

of kinesthesia to language—proposing that all language creates a visceral connection with our feelings and senses, and embeds within us like muscle memory. This is the true power of great poetry and prose. We read John Ciardi's *How Does a Poem Mean?*, which instructed us not just to read poetry, but to read it *aloud*, so that we could feel the poet's intention through not only the word choices, but through rhythm and cadence. This is yet another way we enlarge our imaginations and cultivate wonder. Reading aloud is a shared experience. One speaks, the other listens.

In each class with Professor Lee, we read aloud from the great poets—as many as we could. We read everything from the great lamentation of Shakespeare's King Lear ("Never, never, never, never, never") to John Keats ("Beauty is truth, truth beauty—that is all ye know on earth, and all ye need to know") to Dylan Thomas ("Do not go gentle into that good night. Rage, rage against the dying of the light") to E. E. Cummings ("anyone lived in a pretty how town") to Emily Dickinson ("Because I could not stop for Death—He kindly stopped for me").

There were many others—far too many to list here—but after each class, we all came away almost levitating. I was quite simply inspired in a way that no other course I've ever taken has inspired me, and I think it was because we had listened to and shared the realms of great minds *out loud*.

The great poets give me "ears to hear." I learned to listen to how they built their ideas with the musicality of language, cadence, and rhyme structure, and how all of that comes together in elegant precision in order to create the poem's full intent.

In the Tennyson poem quoted at the beginning of this chapter, he masterfully creates the sound and feeling of bells ringing wildly. In the first line, "Ring out, wild bells, to the wild sky," twice the word *wild* uplifts, as if the up and down forces of the bells themselves are catapulting the bells higher and higher. Each subsequent line sounds and feels like the to and fro of church bells in riotous joy . . . Until the very last line of the verses reproduced here: "Ring in the common love of good." Then the cadence slows down, as if the bell ringer is letting go of each pull and the bells slow to a halt.

As I mentioned earlier in this book, my favorite sound memory from my childhood was the closing *thwack* of a porch screen door on a hot summer's evening. Once the latch shut, it meant you were in for the night. But then came the advent of air conditioning and double-glazed glass, and that sound went away with my childhood. Somehow it haunted me, though. I knew that sound was unique to that time and place in my childhood.

A couple of years ago, I took a week's retreat at the Abbey of Gethsemani in Bardstown, Kentucky—famously the spiritual home of poet, social activist, and prolific author Thomas Merton. In the mid-nineteenth century, French Trappist Monks had bought two thousand acres in the woodlands of Kentucky and built their monastery there throughout the Civil War. Merton converted to Catholicism in the 1930s and entered the abbey in 1941, where he was ordained as Father Louis.

During the week, we were all obliged to go about our daily life in silence. After a friend of mine arranged a meeting between myself and Brother Paul—who had been a novice under Merton—we met in a side office and were free to talk. Brother Paul asked me if I would like to visit Merton's hermitage, where he had lived on the outskirts of the abbey's woodlands in the last years of his life. I was deeply honored and said, "Of course, I would love to."

We drove down a dusty country lane, far into the woods, until we came upon a very humble two-room cement-block home with a simple front porch. Inside, set before a wide window looking out on a clearing in the forest, sat Merton's desk where he wrote, prayed, and meditated. In the center of the room stood a wood-burning stove, and along the walls were shelves filled with Merton's diaries. The second room was a primitive kitchen with a hot plate and a simple bed. Off to the side was Merton's own chapel, where he took the daily Eucharist. I was deeply moved that I could sit at his desk and look out at his view, which I imagined had remained relatively unchanged since his passing in 1968, while on a trip to Bangkok to appeal for interfaith understanding between Buddhists and Christians. Very few people were given this opportunity to be here.

Then we walked out the front screen door and *I heard it*. A subtle screech, the *thwack*. Merton's screen door. I waited for it to close. Brother Paul asked me why I was staring at it. I told him I was astonished to hear this childhood memory come alive. He said, "Well, that screen door was here when Merton was, no doubt about it. He would have heard it, too."

Each sound—like a snowflake—is unique. Sound waves are living; they only exist in time as it's passing. The knowledge that that particular sound had been heard daily by Merton made me feel that somehow we were connected.

So far I have put a lot of emphasis on sound, but where does this connect with people who are deaf or hard of hearing? I have met with several vibrant actors from Tony-nominated Deaf West Theatre in Los Angeles, and they spoke with disdain of the "hearing world's" belief that all deaf people want cochlear implants that would allow them to experience the world of audible sound. I'll bet many of us have watched and wept happily at the YouTube videos of the moving, teary reactions of formerly deaf people hearing for the very first time once the cochlear implant is turned on, and although there is no doubt that this is an electrifying, mind-blowing experience for those who elect to have the procedure, the actors I met say that they themselves "hear" just fine—because they "listen" with full attention to each other. They connect and thrive as deaf people, and they love the beauty and expressiveness of signing. One thing I noticed being in a room full of deaf individuals passionately signing is that they are fully focused on each other—looking, observing, and reacting. They take each other in with kindness and courtesy. In fact, I felt like the outsider that I was, sure that I was missing out on their great camaraderie.

Dame Evelyn Glennie, the Scottish virtuoso percussionist, became virtually deaf at age twelve and thereafter taught herself to hear with parts of her body other than her ears. In her 2003 TED Talk, "How to Truly Listen," she said, "My aim really is to teach the world to listen. That's my only real aim in life." She now performs worldwide, saying, "We're all connected by sound." When she lost her hearing, she was fortunate to find a music teacher who could teach her to listen through her body. She mastered a range of percussion instruments—including the xylophone, snare drum, timpani, and even the Great Highland bagpipes—by, first of all, taking off her shoes and listening through her bare feet, using vibrations to interpret the sounds.

She became accomplished through years of practice, and yet when she applied to the Royal Academy of Music in London, she was roundly dismissed. They told her they could not support her because they knew of no career she could have as a deaf musician. But Glennie and her family prevailed in the end—appealing her admission on the terms that every entrant had *the right to be heard*, and then accepted or rejected based on their musical ability alone. After her second audition, she was accepted, and the RAM opened its doors to people with disabilities of all types. Today, Glennie has an illustrious career, which includes performing solo concerts and with orchestras all over the world. Indeed, she made a dramatic entrance at the opening ceremony of the London 2012 Olympic Games when she led one thousand drummers into the arena.

Evelyn Glennie's success has furthered the cause of inclusivity and opened doors for others coming after her, but she is is still what we would call an "outlier." She is not typical; she has pushed the envelope and done extraordinary things.

Yet it is the derring-do of society's outliers that have helped civilization advance. The outliers are the visionary thinkers, artists, and rebels, the adventurers who seek out new realms. The outliers dare others to listen to their point of view—which, of course, can feel threatening to mainstream society *because it's a new idea.*

Since time immemorial, it was the outlier who made the decision to leave their own tribe, traipse through wild, uncharted territory, and venture into foreign enclaves. Imagine how that group felt when they saw this stranger. If they killed him, well, the story is over. But when the hosts and the newcomers dared to meet around the campfire and listen—they would invariably find new common ground, even if they didn't know each other's language. The outlier would show them, perhaps, his sack full of berries: "Hey, we found a use for these berries. Try this."

Or draw in the mud: "There's a great plain two valleys away full of game and wild boars." Or demonstrate: "We learned how to heal this illness by using this poultice."

> Never question the wisdom of what you fail to understand, for the world is filled with wonders.

L. Frank Baum, *The Wonderful Wizard of Oz*

Listening is to wonder as breathing is to life. To listen well, you open yourself to the other person, you give them your attention and your time. You are taken on a journey. And if you've listened well, you're never quite the same again. Your life horizons will expand.

To thrive we must cultivate wonder. When we despair, grow cynical and snarky, and self-select our own filter bubbles, we diminish our capacity. We become smug, self-satisfied know-it-alls; "been there, done that."

Perhaps the hardest thing to do as we grow up and grow older is to stay young and curious. Cultivating wonder is as essential to our well-being as eating well, exercising, and loving well.

In his 1992 book of daily meditations, *Listening to Your Life*, Presbyterian minister and Pulitzer Prize finalist Frederick Buechner tells the story of a great theologian who was lecturing at length on the subject of miracles. When he was challenged to name one miracle he had personally experienced, he replied, "There is only one miracle. It is life."

Buechner goes on to ask readers the following questions:

Have you wept at anything during the past year?
Has your heart beat faster at the sight of young beauty?
Have you thought seriously about the fact that someday
you are going to die?
More often than not, do you really *listen* when people
are speaking to you instead of just waiting for your
turn to speak?

One young woman had similar advice to share. Holly
Butcher, a twenty-seven-year-old from New South Wales,
Australia, died on January 4, 2018, from Ewing's sarcoma, a
rare form of bone cancer. Among many wise offerings from
those who have been given the gift of knowing their days
are numbered, she left behind an open letter to the world,
which she asked her family to post on Facebook after her
death. In it, she says:

Get up early sometimes and listen to the birds while
you watch the beautiful colours the sun makes as it
rises. Listen to music. Really listen. Music is therapy.
Old is best. Talk to your friends. Put down your phone.
Are they doing okay? Tell your loved ones you love
them every time you get the chance and love them
with everything you have.

In the course of writing this book, I've been repeatedly struck by the fact that the word *listen* is often the last
word in a sentence—a kind of final surrender or a noble
bow. And there *is* something noble about it. Somehow, by
listening and not returning fire with fire, we move on to a
kinder and more mature place of understanding. Such is
the power of listening well: we experience truth. And we

flourish for it—our hearts expand, our minds burst open—creating one fleeting touch point in our briefly crossing orbits.

Listening only occurs in time. Take the time. Each moment we listen creates a common good. Let us all do this one good thing: listen.

Being heard is so close to being loved that for the average person, they are almost indistinguishable.

David Augsburger

Resources

Watch

Documentaries

Alive Inside: A Story of Music and Memory, directed by Michael Rossato-Bennett (2014), Netflix

The Art of Listening, directed by Michael Coleman and Emmanuel Moran (2017), theartoflisteningfilm.com

Making Waves: The Art of Cinematic Sound, directed by Midge Costin (to be released 2018)

Films

Here is an incomplete selection of films with masterful sound design. When you view a classic film, keep in mind the words of Francis Ford Coppola: "Sound is 50 percent of the experience."

2001: A Space Odyssey, directed by Stanley Kubrick

American Graffiti, directed by George Lucas, sound by Walter Murch

Apocalypse Now, directed by Francis Ford Coppola, sound by Walter Murch

The Birds, directed by Alfred Hitchcock

Blade Runner, directed by Ridley Scott

Blue Velvet, directed by David Lynch, sound by Alan Splet

Braveheart, directed by Mel Gibson, sound by Anna Behlmer

Breathless, directed by Jean-Luc Godard

Citizen Kane, directed by Orson Welles

A Clockwork Orange, directed by Stanley Kubrick

The Conversation, directed by Francis Ford Coppola, sound by Walter Murch

The Elephant Man, directed by David Lynch, sound by Alan Splet

Eraserhead, directed by David Lynch, sound by Alan Splet

ET, directed by Steven Spielberg, sound by Ben Burtt

Finding Nemo, directed by Andrew Stanton, sound by Gary Rydstrom

Gladiator, directed by Ridley Scott, sound by Karen Baker Landers and Per Hallberg

The Godfather and *The Godfather Part II*, directed by Francis Ford Coppola, sound by Walter Murch

Gravity, directed by Alfonso Cuarón, sound by Glenn Freemantle

Inside Out, directed by Pete Docter, sound by Ren Klyce

Jurassic Park, directed by Steven Spielberg, sound by Gary Rydstrom

Lincoln, directed by Steven Spielberg, sound by Gary Rydstrom and Ben Burtt

Luxo Jr., directed by John Lasseter, sound by Gary Rydstrom

Mad Max: Fury Road, directed by George Miller, sound by Mark Mangini

Ordinary People, directed by Robert Redford, sound by Kay Rose

Raging Bull, directed by Martin Scorsese, sound by Frank Warner

Rear Window, directed by Alfred Hitchcock

A River Runs Through It, directed by Robert Redford, sound by Gary Rydstrom

Saving Private Ryan, directed by Steven Spielberg, sound by Gary Rydstrom

Schindler's List, directed by Steven Spielberg

The Social Network, directed by David Fincher, sound by Ren Klyce

Spartacus, directed by Stanley Kubrick

A Star Is Born, directed by Frank Pierson, sound overseen by Barbara Streisand

Star Wars: Episodes IV, V, and VI, directed by George Lucas, sound by Ben Burtt

Tin Toy, directed by John Lasseter, sound by Gary Rydstrom

Toy Story 1, 2, and 3, directed by John Lasseter, sound by Gary Rydstrom

Trainspotting, directed by Danny Boyle

Up, directed by Pete Docter, sound by Tom Myers

Wall-E, directed by Andrew Stanton, sound by Ben Burtt

Listen

Radio

Across the Red Line, BBC Radio Four

Ted Talks (ted.com)

Evelyn Glennie, "How To Truly Listen"

Bernie Krause, "The Voice of The Natural World"

Julian Treasure (various)

Read

Books

The Great Animal Orchestra: Finding the Origins of Music in the World's Wild Places, by Bernie Krause

A Listening Ear, by Paul Tournier

Listening to Your Life: Daily Meditations with Frederick Buechner

On Becoming a Person: A Therapist's View of Psychotherapy, by Carl R. Rogers

Seven Thousand Ways to Listen: Staying Close to What Is Sacred, by Mark Nepo

Articles

Psychology Today: "The Key to Intimacy Is Radical Listening," by Nancy Colier

TheGuardian.com: "The 10 Best Recordings of Poets" (including Alfred, Lord Tennyson; W. H. Auden, Sylvia Plath, Philip Larkin, and Alice Oswald)

Smithsonianmag.com: "Marian Anderson Singing at the Lincoln Memorial, April 9, 1939"

Thanks

To the students and participants in all my story classes worldwide, you taught me the joy of listening. I have flourished and am far better for having heard your stories.

To all my friends around the world—the tall ships, stable and able, in their journeys—Armando Fumagalli, Mara and Alessandro Perbellini, Brian Eastman and Christabel Alberry, David and Clare Hieatt, and the Do community. To the friends who define longevity and constancy: M'Leigh Koziol, Chuck Slocum, Karen Johnson, Carla Brewington, and Lynn Schweitzer-Hudson. My dear beloved family: Eric and Melissa, Margie, Mark and Rachelle, Madison, Morgan, Gianna, Philip, Joseph, and Robbie. And my wonderful support, Jody Berges.

To my editor and publisher, Miranda West—spitfire, the very definition of *command*, a general among us. Thank you for listening to what others have said about my workshops and lectures, and asking me to fulfill this great task.

About the Author

Bobette Buster is the author of *Do Story: How to Tell Your Story So the World Listens* (published by Do Books in the U.K. in 2013 and Chronicle Books in the United States in 2018). She is also the writer and producer of the feature documentary *Making Waves: The Art of Cinematic Sound* (2018) and several feature narrative projects, including *Charlotte* and *Gold Fellas*.

She is a story consultant to leading production companies and major studios including Pixar, Disney, and Sony Animation, as well as to advertising and marketing agencies around the world.

She has lectured internationally and is currently a professor of digital storytelling at Northeastern University, in Boston.

She lives in Los Angeles, California.

Connect with Bobette on Twitter at @bobettebuster or via her website, bobettebuster.com.

Index

Notes

Books in the series:

Do Breathe
Calm your mind. Find focus.
Get stuff done.
Michael Townsend Williams

Do Disrupt
Change the status quo. Or become it.
Mark Shayler

Do Fly
Find your way. Make a living.
Be your best self.
Gavin Strange

Do Grow
Start with 10 simple vegetables.
Alice Holden

Do Purpose
Why brands with a purpose do better
and matter more.
David Hieatt

Do Story
How to tell your story so the world listens.
Bobette Buster

A percentage of royalties from each
copy sold will go to the DO Lectures,
a workshop series for sharing ideas
and inspiring action.

For more in the DO Books series,
visit **www.chroniclebooks.com.**

To learn more about DO Lectures,
visit **www.thedolectures.com.**